How to be an Expired Master

By

Jason Morris

Table of Content

About Me	6
Disclaimer	8
Introduction	9
What is an Expired?	10
How do you contact Expireds?	11
How your expired listing business Should look	16
Misconceptions and BS excuses	24
Why should Agents work with expired leads?	31
Why do listings expire?	34
But Expired Sellers are so Mean!	49
Scripts	54
Expired Script	59
Your pre-listing package	61
Building your follow up system	69
Using a Pricing Strategy	88
Setting up your net sheet	93
Listing Paperwork Presentation	99
Listing appointment	105
Putting my whole system together	115

Tools and tips to Make this easier	118
Bonus: The $100,000 notebook plan	122
Other expired Contact and Follow up Ideas	129
Thank You	132

Do you want to take more expired listing?

Do you want to build a listing heavy business?

Do you want to take back control of your time and your life?

Do you want a more predictable income?

Of course you do….. That is why you bought this book!

Until January 1, 2020 when you join my group coaching and you use the code "ExpiredBook" the first month will only be $7!! Go to www.JasonMorrisGroupCoaching.com and enter the code at the check out

About Me

If you are reading this report, you probably know me from my youtube videos or my Facebook group "Real Estate Agents that REALLY work". If you are not in my Facebook group, go join today!

I have been a real estate agent for 16 years. Here is the short version of my story.

I started selling real estate when I was right out of college. I was the very definition of a broke college kid. I worked a full time job from 4pm until midnight and sold real estate from 8am until I had to get ready for work at 4pm. It sucked… I didn't have a sphere of influence, didn't have money for marketing and worked at an office with NO training. My first 6 months, I was just thrown in the business and had to figure it out.

A few years later, I started a team, won a bunch of awards and realized working as close to 24 hours a day, 7 days a week as I possibly could, really sucked. I am pretty sure I had a stomach ulcer, plus I really wasn't making very much money. I had a lot of expensive systems, assistants and stuff that was supported by bits and pieces of a lot of transactions and stress!

A couple of years after that I decided to disband the team, I got divorced and went back to being a single agent. I rebuilt my business in a way that supported the lifestyle I wanted to have. I wanted a business that was highly profitable, not much overhead, afternoons and weekends off and I didn't want to have to worry about my phone while I was trying to do stuff that I wanted to do! I created that business model for myself. A business that worked for me and the lifestyle I wanted.

So in 2019, I train real estate agents to do exactly what I did, build highly predictable businesses with low overhead and a schedule that works for them.

I teach you how to make your business work for you, not you work for your business.

You can find out more at
www.JasonMorrisGroupCoaching.com

Jason Morris

Disclaimer

This whole document is from my experience in the real estate business prospecting FSBOs and Expireds. Hopefully you get a few ideas from it or learn to get over some misconceptions around prospecting expired listings.

I have performed minimal editing and proofreading in this document.

It was put together by me personally, for your benefit. I didn't put this together for me, I did it for you. I hope it helps your business.

If you find a misspelled word, missing comma etc please print out your copy, use some white out and correct it on your version. I am sure there are a few mistakes in the next few pages.

None of this information in this book is a guarantee, its all based on my experience and requires you to work.

Introduction

Having coached thousands of real estate agents in the last few years there are often these ideas and stereotypes about why listings expire from MLS.

Most agents not prospecting expired listings believe that the only reason the property expired was because it was over priced. So they have this idea of "I am not calling them, they are asking too much."

I wrote this book to give new and experienced real estate agents a guide for going out and working with sellers who have a property that expired from MLS.

The goal of this book is to help you understand the mindset of a seller who just had a property expire and to give you a system to cost effectively build a business or a profit center for your business from this high quality lead source.

Feel free to share this with other agents needing help.

What is an Expired?

When I am writing about an "expired" in this book, I am simply talking about a property that has expired from the Multiple Listing Service (MLS) in your local market.

In a normal market, listings expire everyday. In an up market like we have had the last few years this lead source has not been as plentiful. Don't worry the market moves in cycles, just because you do not have many expireds to call today, that could change soon.

How do you contact Expireds?

This is a great question. I get it all of the time.

Of course you can go on your MLS and pull a list of the expired listings every. Its easy and it's free to do that with your MLS subscription.

The problem is, the MLS sheets have all the property information on them, but _they do not have the property owner's contact information_. There is not any easy way to get their contact information on your own. Of course you can try to find them on facebook, try looking them up on Google etc, but it is tough to find them and time consuming.

The harder you make it to get expired listing contact data, the least like it is that you will consistently do it. When I first started prospecting expireds, I was hard headed and (if you know me) sometimes I try to be cheap. I would spend 3 or 4 hours at night looking up numbers to make calls the next day for an hour. It was a ton of work!

It is a lot easier to just open up your laptop, login to a website and have number waiting on you to start dialing.

One thing I do want to make sure you know is, all expired contact data is mined data. This means that someone (or a software algorithm) has to sort through massive databases looking for contact data that correlates to specific address.

Any company that tells you that their expired data is 100% accurate is not telling you the truth. In 2019, it is not possible to get 100% accurate contact information for every listing in your market that expires. This is where some agents get discouraged. You will get wrong numbers.

However, you will get wrong numbers if you are running facebook ads, buying leads from Zillow or just doing SEO on your own person website. It is just part of doing sales.

The best way to get expired data and contact information is to pay for it through a reputable company like Redx. I have been using Redx since they first came out offering expired contact data. Everytime I switched, I ended up switching back. You can get a discount subscribing at www.JasonMorrisexpiredleads.com

Redx offers 2 different products for expired listings. The first product is just the regular expired numbers and is a little lower cost. I would recommend this for agents just starting out prospecting. This data has been collected using an algorithm and has been scored to be phone numbers that are possibly the correct number for your home seller.

The second product they offer is a premium expired data product called "Onyx". With this subscription they give you 100% of the data they can find that correlates with a specific address. There are a few advantages with getting this subscription. The first one is, you will get all of the numbers they can find. By sorting through this data yourself you will find a lot of hard to get phone numbers that no one else can easily get. You also email addresses (I will give you some ideas on how you can use these in a later chapter).

The downside of using Onyx for agents new to prospecting is, you get a LOT of data. To be the most effective with this subscription, you need to make sure that you use a dialer. Redx provides a CRM as part of all of their subscriptions that you can use to sort through the data.

Take a look at the next chapter and I will explain how your business and system will look and I will include a graphic.

How your expired listing business Should look

Level 1 — First conversation

Level 2 — Follow up with correct number

Level 3 — Long term following plan

Level 4 — Listing appointments

Signed listing agreements

So this really sums up the purpose of this book, in 1 picture. You see the bucket dumping expired data into the top of your funnel? (You say "yes).

That is the data that you are getting from Redx or you are looking up yourself. For this system to work, you have to have expired listing sellers to call. If you don't have anything to pour into the top of your funnel, nothing will ever come out of the bottom.

There are 4 lead levels. I want to explain each one to you, so you have a complete understanding of what is going to happen in this process. In one of the later chapters, we will talk about some tools to assist you better in working your leads through the funnel faster. I don't want to bog you down into thinking you need a lot of stuff to get started. I prospected for years with nothing more than leads, a cell phone and a spiral notebook.

Level 1. First conversation calls
This very top level of the funnel is big! Really, the bigger the better. On these calls you are weeding out bad numbers, properties that were re-listed, properties that were sold but not updated and hopefully you are having a few good conversations with sellers still looking to sell.

If it you get a bad number, just delete them. If you get an angry seller don't worry about it, we will talk about why they are angry later in the book, but you want to keep all correct contact information and people you had conversations with.

Level 2. Following up with sellers and correct Numbers

The people you talked to and correct phone numbers, you want to keep calling them. At this level you are looking for meaningful conversations. These are conversations where they really tell you personal stuff. Things like exactly why they are selling, why their last agent didn't sell their house, exactly what price they are willing to accept and whatever else they are willing to volunteer. You are looking for motivated sellers. People who want to do something with their homes soon.

When you have these meaningful conversations these motivated sellers, these leads move down to Level 3.

Level 3. Long term Follow up

Level 3 is where things really good. Only a small percentage of your leads will get here. If you haven't noticed, the funnels is longer for this level, but not nearly as wide. This is on purpose. These people want to do something with their property and they want to do it soon.

These are your most important leads. I would print these leads off of your crm and put them in a folder, notebook or 3 ring binder. You want to make sure you consistently following up with these people.

I would set up a plan to make a minimum of 12 to 15 (or more) follow up attempts with these sellers. I created my Follow up Master Day Planner www.FollowupMasterDayPlanner.com , for this specific purpose. It gives agents a full years worth of seller follow up tips and ideas. It is available on Amazon.

Personally, I like printing these people off and putting them in a notebook at this stage. You can get a copy of my lead sheet by going to www.JasonMorrisBonus.com . One thing I liked to do was write in the top corner of each lead how much commission I would make, as a listing agent, if I listed and sold their property. Can you imagine walking around with a notebook that has 30 to 40 hot seller leads in it? That are worth an estimated $3,000 to $5,000 each? or more depending on you market? That is easily over six figures of future potential income.

How many agents are walking around with a notebook that contains $100,000+ of highly potential future business?

I am including a chapter in the end of this book to help you get ramped up quickly to that level of future potential income.

The goal is with level 3 leads to set listing appointments. I can not stress enough, follow up is what is going to make or break your whole expired listing business. Most agents maybe follow up 1 time? Maybe 2 times? No one follows up continuously, keeping sellers informed about what is happening in the market.

I never heard a seller say "I didn't list my home with (insert agent name), they just followed up with me too much and kept me too informed". Usually it is the opposite, "I talked to them one time and then never heard from them again.

Level 4. The Listing appointment
In this book, I am outlining all of the tools and things you need for the listing appointment to make sure you show up and have the best possible chance of listing their home.

Here is where level 4 gets a little tricky, you are meeting these sellers, in most cases face to face. This is the highest level of seller lead you can possibly have, sellers that want to sell their house and have actually met you! After this, they know you. They are probably going to recognize you if they see you out to dinner or in the grocery store.

If they do not sign your listing paperwork, they go back to level 3, but they are the best lead you can have. You need to follow up with them continuously.

Most agents will show up to a listing appointment, then if they don't leave with paperwork signed, they never follow up again.

One thing I can tell you for sure is, sometimes I have met people about buying a product or service and I was really excited about it. The reason I didn't sign up was….. I just was not ready yet. Maybe Monday afternoon was a good day to meet, but it just was not a good day to get started.

I have done that exact same thing, I am sure you have also.

Sometimes, the reason they didn't sign the listing paperwork with you that day was really the exact reason they gave you. They were just not ready yet.

The Listing Appointment

Hopefully, by the time you show up at the house you have already ready started your sales process. Here is what you sales process should look like

1. Send pre-listing package
2. Follow up to make sure they received the pre-listing package
3. Put together your pricing strategy
4. Put together your net sheet

5. Put together all paperwork (listing paperwork) and supported documents
6. Show up to the appointment about 10 to 15 minutes early!
7. View the house
8. Go over your pricing strategy, net sheet and paperwork

In this book we are going to go over each section of your sales process, so that you can put together your own sales system that will highly convert listings.

Misconceptions and BS excuses

I want to eliminate as many of your excuses as possible. Most of the reasons you are not prospecting expireds are just excuses. These excuses are stealing your dreams and preventing you from hitting your goals. Your excuses are taking away the things you want.

They are taking things away from you and your family. You are only 1 to 2 expired listing sales away from SO MANY GOALS!!

Want a new car?
Want to take the kids to Disney World?
Want a bigger house?
Want to have more money in the bank?

Follow the information I am giving you in this book and take a couple extra listings by prospecting expired leads!

They are not angry at you, they are angry at their situation!

There really is not 50 agents calling them every day! Even if there is, most of those agents suck, they have no script, no follow up system and they get 1 BS objection and they throw the seller's contact information away.

You have agents right now in your office that say things like:
"Calling expireds doesn't work"
"Expired sellers are mean"
"I would never do that"
"All the numbers are wrong"

Those agents are typically broke and are probably selling just enough to tread water!

If you look at the top agents and superstars in the real estate business, across the United States, just about everyone of them has a system for expired leads.

You have the opportunity of a lifetime! You have the golden ticket. This book is a treasure map! You just need to go dig up the treasure!

Do not let the mindset and opinions of others rob you of your success!

7 Reasons Most agents fail with Expired sellers

1. <u>They never actually call enough expired listings and sellers in general to get really</u>

good at the process of taking listings.

It is like playing golf, if you play only one time a year, you are not going to be very good. If you play a few times a week and practice everyday, your skill level will increase rapidly.

2. They don't use a script.

I hear it all the time from agents, "I don't like scripts". The problem is, if we just get on the phone and say whatever we want to say, sometimes we don't know what is going to come out of our mouths.

The magic with using a script is, once we ask those same 5 to 7 questions to 50 sellers, 100 sellers, 1,000 sellers we are going to know all the answers to those questions and all the objections. After a while, you get so good at knowing the answers to those questions that you can almost anticipate them and overcome objections before you even get them! Its like you are developing psychic powers!

3. They have no sales process.

We are working in a sales business that has a problem with actually learning a sales process. So many agents want to call themselves anything other than "salesmen/saleswomen".

We have agents talking about how they are property experts, marketers, consultants or whatever title you can think of. But they have no consistent process to handle any lead at all. They just kind of float around and "hope" something will happen.

Just because you subscribe to a lead source or system, that does not mean clients are going to start falling into your lap with pre-printed contracts and hoping they can put your name in the empty agent blanks.

New Business happens consistently when you consistently perform a process that brings in new business. Want to work with more home sellers? Easy, talk to more people thinking about selling a home.

4. <u>They keep talking to sellers about "listing" their house.</u>

"Hey, let me list your house." "hey Mr Seller, I would love to list your house." "I can list your house."

There is a problem with using the term "listing". The problem is, it is just industry slang and outside of our industry it has a negative connotation. Typically, you only hear the word when people use it in phrases like "I listed my house, but it didn't sell" or "I listed my house and they agent never called me again".

I promise you, these sellers want to "sell" their house not "list" their house. If you change your conversations where you talk about "selling" their house, your conversations will change instantly.

5. They NEVER follow up! Never!!

   Most agent never follow up. Some never make the first call! When I first published my "Follow up Master Day Planner" www.FollowupMasterDayPlanner.com , agents thought it was magical, no one talked about follow up in our industry.

   In the book, The Ultimate Sales Machine, Chet Holmes talks about luxury products take 6 to 8 follow up attempts before someone bought or used their services. So when he designed sales systems while working for Fortune 500 companies they typically included as many as 15 to 17 sales follow ups.

   With all of the money that many of these

companies spend researching and tracking their sales, as agents we should design massive follow up systems for our businesses also.

6. <u>They have horrible posture on the phone.</u>

Posture is the belief in what you are doing, regardless of outside acceptance or approval. This belief and confidence shines through and I think can actually be felt over the phone. Many of you might be extremely confident, however the tone of your voice and the words you use do not sound very confident.

I think with improving tonality used during your calls, the biggest thing you can work on is self awareness. It wouldn't hurt to regularly record your calls and listen back to them.

Also listen to the way you phrase your words. Think about this, if you had a major medical problem, would you rather go to the doctor that "thinks he can fix your problem" and talks really low and soft or the one that "Knows they can fix your problem" and they sound strong and confident?

7. <u>They never offer value.</u>

   Most agents are calling and it is a 100% self serving call. They offer no value whatsoever. They are basically calling and saying "Hey you want to sell your house?". If the person says no, they hang up and dial the next number.

   They never ask the seller questions and they never provide answers to any of the questions the sellers ask.

   The best way to add value to a conversation is by asking questions, having MLS pulled up and giving information to sellers that may improve their situation or knowledge about their situation.

Why should Agents work with expired leads?

This is a great question I have been asked by agents in my coaching program. I believe this is one of the highest quality lead sources we can easily get our hands on. One of the only other lead sources that compare to prospecting expired listings would be FSBOs. You can check out my book "How to be a FSBO Master" on Amazon.

Here are a few reasons why you should be contacting expired listings

1. We know they want to sell their property (or at least wanted to sell their property). It has openly been on the market, in most cases from 3 to 6 months. They are not just thinking about it, they have already taken action on it.

2. We know they are open to working with a real estate agent and are willing to pay a commission. They just ended a relationship with an agent, they were more than likely

offering a commission to.

3. We have more information available on these leads than any other lead source. Think about this. Someone that signs up on your website, typically you have limited information. A for sale by owner lead, the ad only has a limited amount of information.

   An expired listing, we have pictures, a description, tax information, price adjustment information and just about every detail you can have and it was provided by the previous listing agent.

4. This lead source is virtually unlimited! Some of you might only get a couple a day, but I'm almost certain you can go back in your MLS and get thousands of old leads from the last few months or even the last couple of years.

There is not another lead source to prospect that we know so much about. Even your sphere of influence, as great of a lead source as it can be is limited. Your brother, cousin and co-workers will only send you so many potential leads a month/year. However, expireds just keep coming!

Why do listings expire?

Well the easy answer many times is, they were just over priced. Either the seller just wanted too much for the property or the agent just didn't educate the seller on what was really happening in the market.

This is not always the case.

I made a list of 10 reasons with some stories from my real estate experience of other reasons why listings expire. I want you to understand it is not always price. Of course price can typically overcome most issues. The seller can't always accept the price needed to overcome a problem, sometimes the price is just too low. This is when you have to figure out exactly what the problem is.

People don't often sell their home and move on a whim or because they didn't have anything to do last weekend. I have always felt like most sellers are selling their property because they have a problem and typically they think selling will fix it. They could be upsizing, downsizing, in foreclosure, moving for a job, etc, but they have something that is an issue for them.

Over the last 16 years I have learned that a lot of expired sellers have a 2nd problem. Usually it is one the 1st listing agent did not identify. That is why they couldn't sell their house. That is why the house appeared to be a pretty fair price but after months of having it listed with an agent, nothing happened.

I believe that one of the highest paid skills you can learn in the real estate industry is identifying problems and figuring out how to fix them for sellers.

Here is a list of 10 other reasons homes expire from MLS.

#1 Bad pictures or wrong pictures

Now, I am not an advocate for professional photography, drone footage etc on every single listing. I believe you can buy a decent camera with a wide angle lense and take pictures that would be the equivalent of most of the professional real estate photographers.

One reason I have taken my own pictures in the past is because I could get their home on MLS the same day we sign a listing agreement. If I hired a photographer it might take a week just to get an appointment for pictures.

I think as long as the pictures look good and accurately show the home, they are sufficient in most cases.

I have seen in the past agents having bad pictures (or even the wrong pictures) being a major problem when putting a home on MLS.

One day I was following up with an expired seller. The second call with her, she started telling me about all the upgrades she made to her condo. As she was listing these items off, she mentioned new kitchen cabinets, granite countertops, hardwood floors, crown molding and she had the place painted after she moved out.

I pulled up the listing while I was on the phone with her and was scrolling through the pictures, I realized I was not seeing these upgrades in the pictures. A matter of fact, The pictures were showing old kitchen cabinets, carpet in the living room and a lot of furniture. She was telling me it was empty when she put it on the market.

Turns out the listing agent had her home on the market for 6 months, had her do 2 price reductions and had really bad pictures of the wrong condo on MLS!

I re-listed her condo for her original asking price, with correct pictures and a list of the upgrades I had an accepted contract within 30 days.

#2 Bad description or No Description

When we put a property on MLS, we really only have 2 ways to make the listing stand out. We have pictures and a description. This is the first impression the general public sees of the house. Bad Pictures and a Bad descripts and they just hit the next button when looking at houses.

I was making my follow up calls one day and was talking to a lady that I could tell was really motivated to sell her house. It was with another agent for 3 months and expired.

Looking at the listing it looked way overpriced. Talking to the seller, she really couldn't come down much if any on the price. I stuck to my script and asked more questions about the features of the home and I set an appointment.

There was one odd thing when I was preparing for the appointment. All of the homes in the neighborhood had garages, except hers. With a garage it was priced where it needed to be, without a garage it was about $25,000 over priced. Which is a lot on a $150,000 home.

I went through MLS and found the old listing where she bought the home, guess what… the home had a garage! The listing agent left it out of the listing and did not have 1 picture showing a 2 car garage! Talk about missing a major, important feature of the home!

I showed up to the appointment with the expired MLS sheet. Turns out not only did the agent not put the garage in the listing, they didn't mention a huge sunroom, a fenced in backyard and the fact the home backed up to the woods.

These were all huge advantages over other listings in the neighborhood. We listed the home for the exact price as the previous agent and had a contract within a week.

#3 Their home was too hard to show

I think we have all had this problem before when showing buyers houses. It didn't matter what time we requested, it was like we just could not get a showing approved. Well chances are you were not the only agent that had this problem.

Every now and then there will be a well priced home that is just tough to show. Maybe the home has a tenant in it or a seller that just does not want to cooperate with showings.

The problem most agents have is they will not have a serious heart to heart conversation with the seller and tell them "if you can't show the house, you can't sell the house".

I had a property I listed one time, the sellers were out of state and they inherited the house after their mom passed away. The issue was, after mom died, some of her friends moved in the house! Originally they started out as tenants, eventually they quit paying rent. They hadn't paid rent in over a year and the sellers didn't want to evict them. When I went over to the house, they told me they were related and they were looking for a place to move.

When we set up showings it was a different story. The people living there would confirm the appointment with me and when the buyers agent would show up they would tell them "you are at the wrong house" or "oh, that agent made a mistake this house isn't for sale."

After this happened a few times, I figured out what was going on. I called the sellers, talked to them about the issue. Of course the people living in the house denied it. The sellers would still not evict them or tell them they had to leave.

The house didn't sell. As far as I know, the house still has not sold and with the showing situation what it is, it may never sell.

#4 The listing agent never answered their phone

If you have been in the real estate business for a while, I am sure you have had this issue. Dealing with a listing agent who just never responds to anything!!

If the listing agent rarely answers their phone and they never respond to showing request or text, it makes it tough to sell the house.

I was representing a buyer a few years ago. This guy was a pretty educated buyer and reasonable as far as what he was willing to pay.. He was paying cash and pretty much knew exactly where he wanted to live. He was the sort of buyer we hope we get.

I showed up to meet him with 4 houses scheduled to see. We look at them, but there was a 5th one he really wanted to get into but the agent hadn't called me back. I tried calling the agent several times during the time we were looking. He had already walked around house #5, looked through the windows. All 4 houses we looked at, he compared to house #5. The problem is we couldn't get in this house.

He was going to be in town for a few more days and was set on seeing this house. For 3 days, I called this agent, called his office and got no response. The house was empty. There was a private lock box on the house and we didn't have the code. His office didn't have the code either.

The buyer, ended up leaving town, with plans to come back in a week or two. A week later, the agent returns my call! No explanation or anything, just a "hey just got your message". We ended up submitting an offer the house contingent on viewing. My buyer drove here the next day and looked at it, loved the house and closed a couple weeks later.

During those few weeks, I never talked to the listing agent again. He never returned a call, the attorney handled everything.

This house showed great! Was in great shape! It was priced well, but it was on the market for over 5 months. I wonder how many other agents tried to show it?

#5 Difficult Real Estate Agents

Let's be honest, we all have those agents in local markets that are just so hard to deal with! I think a lot of them believe they are the decision maker in the transaction and they never give their seller the opportunity to respond.

We had a foreclosure agent in my market that, I feel sure the bank lost money giving them listings because they were just so difficult to deal with. Anytime you heard their name it was followed with a story about how they were just a jerk.

There was always an issue with the offer, the prequalification letter, the proof of funds or just some random thing.

I would be willing to bet your market has an agent just like this and they have a reputation for being difficult to deal with. I bet their listings often get skipped, when buyers agents are setting up showings.

#6 Difficult sellers

If you take enough listings you will get a seller that is difficult to deal with. All showings have to be on their terms and they are not willing to negotiate on anything at all.

Over the years, I have occasionally had a seller that would end up with several viable offers falling through just because they were so difficult to make a deal with. If the asking price was not an issue, then it would be a closing date or inspection date.

Sometimes, the first offer is the best offer your seller will get. It sucks, but sometimes during the listing time frame you only get one offer and if you don't at least make a counter offer and explore what the buyer is willing to do, you could miss out on an opportunity to sell.

I had a listing that was a house that flooded during a hurricane about 4 years ago. It was an older block house, it had been completely remodeled after the flood and everything was brand new. It hadn't been lived in since being fixed back up. We put it on the market for $75,000 which was a very good price.

We had to disclose it was flooded, but we had a lot of interest. The seller had owned the home for about 15 years and it had never flooded before. We had a lot of showings. The difficult thing was, the homes on the same street still showed signs of being flooded and had piles of trash out front etc. Buyers were a little nervous about buying in that area. Agent feedback confirmed this and the seller was seeing all the feedback requests that were being returned to me.

We finally get an offer for $65,000. The seller would not respond to it! A matter of fact, he called the buyers agent personally and was just a jerk about a "low ball offer". He said he felt like $65,000 was "giving the house away". A few months later my listing expired. Sure enough, a year later the house ended up flooding again! I saw the same house listed on craigslist for $40,000 and it has been on craiglist for a while. If he would have been willing to just throw out a counter offer or showed a willingness to work with the buyer, maybe we could have sold it several years ago.

#7 Acts of God

Sometimes stuff just happens. If you live in the south east, every September for the last 4 or 5 years, we get some sort of hurricane of serious tropical storm.

In the past, I have taken some well priced homes and something would happen and the home just couldn't get shown or the home got torn up by a storm.

About a year ago, we had a Hurricane that hit the coast of North Carolina and it just sat there for a few days dumping rain on the North Carolina coast.

Being just a few miles south in the Myrtle Beach market, it turns out that all that rain water was going to flow in our direction. It was like for 4 to 6 weeks we had bridges out, roads covered with water and a really difficult time just traveling from one place to another. For a little while a drive that would normally be 20 minutes would take hours, if you could even get to where you are going.

You can imagine, there were tons of listings expiring, for no other reason than you couldn't get to them to show them.

This is one example, but I am sure with storm damage, insurance claims and other random acts of god, there are many many more situations where this happens.

#8 Crazy Pets

About 5 year ago, I was following up with a seller. I talked to her several times and I finally set an appointment. When I was doing my research, her property was priced well, maybe even on the low end. However It had expired 3 times and had been on the market for about a year.

I racked my brain looking at all the pictures, comparables and everything asking myself "why did this house expire?"

The day of the listing appointment, I show up and as soon as I pulled up in her yard I see a dog come out from behind the house. I don't know what kind he was, she said he was a "mixed breed". He must have been mixed with a horse because he was one of the biggest dogs I have ever seen. He also did not look friendly AT ALL!!

I was not going to get out of the car. No way would I have let clients get out of the car with this huge dog. I called her and she come outside, she said he was really friendly. It turned out he really was. While looking at the house, this dog followed me around carrying a full sized, partially deflated basketball in his mouth! He was HUGE!

When I sat at her kitchen table, I asked about the 3 previous times the home was on the market and asked if they had any showings. Her response was that people set up appointments, then would pull into the yard and turn around and leave.

Thats when I realized that the problem wasn't the house, the condition or the price it was people were scared of her giant dog. I talked to her about the dog and we came up with a plan on what to do with him during showings.

I put her house on the market and got an offer within a week.

#9 The Homes Condition (or stuff in the home)

Over the years I have seen a lot of stuff going into people's houses. Of course we know that people typically buy based on price, condition and location. There isn't much we can do about the location. Condition can always be an issue we can overcome by cleaning up the house or lowering the price.

The obvious things when it comes to homes being expired would be things like an old roof, flooring, holes in the walls and other damage from wear and tear or just pinterest projects that have gone wrong.

But what about the sellers personal items? Could that turn off buyers looking at the house?

Here are a couple of stories that just came to mind.

I listed a home one time where the seller turned the attic into a 2 chair movie theater. He done a great job, bought expensive stuff to put in it. He was really proud of the home theater too. The problem was, when agents would show it he would have his massive porn dvd collection on display! This guy had hundreds of adult dvds stacked up in the theater room.

I tried to talk to him about it, but he really couldn't see the issue. Every showing we had, I would get a call from the buyers agent wanting to tell me about the theater room.

I had another seller that was an extremely well read person. He was really interesting to talk to also. His home had a massive library. The issue was he liked researching historic, religious rituals. It never failed, everytime his home would have a showing he would have stacks of books on his dining room table that were subjects that were not very friendly. It always resulted in a call from the buyers agent.

#10 The Listing Agents just runs out of time

It happens. You list a home for 90 days, then you get a contract that ties the property up for 60 days before falling apart. Then next thing you know you just run out of time and the seller is discouraged.

This probably happens more than a lot of us will ever understand. Especially, to agents without a lot of experience. The seller signs a 6 month listing agreement and during that time the agent does a few price adjustments or the market picks up. Next thing you know, an overpriced listing is now the cheapest one in the neighborhood, but you are on day 179 of a 180 day listing agreement.

But Expired Sellers are so Mean!

Do you know how many times I have heard agents say things like this? Or had agents give this as an excuse.

I was working at a large office in my market, we had over 125 agents (that is big here). I was the number one listing agent with around 50 listings. I was an individual agent, no team and I was referring my buyer leads out. The office manager kept asking me what I was doing. I kept telling him "calling expired listings and FSBOs every day. He kept telling me how mean they were and how what I was doing was "too hard".

Thankfully, I knew better than to listen. I was spending only about $250 a month on leads, working only about 6 or 7 hours a day and probably netting more income than anyone in the office.

The big difference between him and I was, I am fascinated with asking "why". I felt like I had such an understanding of what was happening in the minds of these leads that I could really help them. I was calling them, because my mindset was that I was their best option.

I think on a basic level we are all the same, just these people you are talking to happen to be lumping you into a somewhat stereotypical view created by their situation and experience with 1 real estate agent.

I mentioned previously, I believe that every seller has a problem, the idea of them selling their house fixes their problem.

I want to share with you what I believe is going on in the mindset of an Expired Seller.

1. **They feel angry and are upset. But it has nothing to do with you**

    Think about it, it sucks when you have been planning something and thinking about something for a while. Then all of a sudden it just does not work out. That is the situation many of these sellers are in. Sometimes all their future plans, hopes and dreams were relying on this property selling.

2. **They feel let down, defeated and maybe lied to. But it has nothing to do with you**

    Have you ever really been relying on someone else to do something but they didn't show up? Maybe someone promised you the world, insured you that something will happen a certain way and it didn't?

That just happened to these sellers.

3. **They feel like they can't depend on anyone**
You ever got really aggravated with someone you hired that just didn't get things right, so you decided you were just going to do it yourself? Maybe it was a landscaper cutting your grass? Maybe it was a painter? Or Maybe you just said, screw this I will just live with whatever it is, like it is.

At different times, I have gotten aggravated with contractors and just decided "I will just do it myself", "None of them show up", or "All of them want to charge a fortune". None of these things are true, there are great contractors out there, just the one or two I was working with, they let me down.

That just happened to these sellers.

The easiest way to explain the feeling is, do you remember back to maybe middle school or high school, when you had that first boyfriend or girlfriend? You loved them, everything was centered around them and what you were going to do together. You couldn't talk to them on the phone enough (we didn't have texting back when I was in high school). But you get the idea?

Then one day, you broke up and you had every emotion you can think or from sadness, anger and finally acceptance. Maybe it took a little while, but you moved on, later found another boyfriend or girlfriend and forgot about the one before.

Maybe not as extreme, but that is the situation with these sellers.

So what do we do about it?

We have to build a sales and follow up process that builds trust and confidence in YOU!!

The rest of this book is going to be about setting up your sales system, so that it is cost effective and it actually works!!

Scripts

I believe using a script is the foundation of prospecting expired listings.

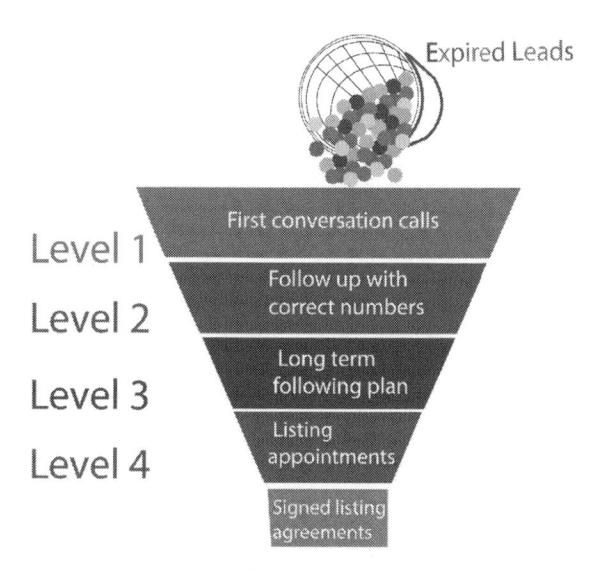

Expired Leads

Level 1 — First conversation calls
Level 2 — Follow up with correct numbers
Level 3 — Long term following plan
Level 4 — Listing appointments

Signed listing agreements

Once you dump your leads into the top of your funnel, the next step is to contact them. I do not recommend contacting them without using a script. You can get a copy of my expired listing script at www.JasonMorrisBonus.com

Using a script is going to do 3 things for you:

1. With a script, you know what to say. You are not fumbling around or talking about

things that are not relevant to the conversation. A script keeps you on track.

2. With a script you know what the seller will say. Once you have asked those same scripted questions over and over, you will quickly here every answer to every question. So after a couple of weeks, you will get to where you can anticipate exactly how a seller will answer every question that you ask.

3. With a script you will have a purpose for every call. Your purpose on the phone is to set an appointment or qualify the lead and move it further down into the follow up process.

When I first started selling real estate I hated using scripts. I had some sales experience from working at Sears when I was in college. I figured, I would just get them on the phone and figure things out from there. It worked for me, but the reason it worked for me was, I was making a massive amount of calls, it was painful!!

Some of my conversations would be about as relevant to selling your house as me asking them "Hey what is your cat doing this afternoon" or "Does your yard have any squirrels?".

Just like I said in one the first sections of this book, agents are going to tell your scripts do not work. Honestly, some of them do not work.

Why some scripts do not work

1. They are just too hard to get through! I have had agents join my coaching program and send me the scripts they were working with. Some of them were using scripts that were extremely long! Some had questions or statements that were just offensive! They had questions that were just not natural questions to ask. The script would never be a part of a natural conversation.

2. Some scripts are using are just over qualifying. They are asking for the seller to commit to listing their home with them before they have even had a real conversation about their house. They are kind of like if you asked someone to marry you before you ever went on a date.

3. The scripts they are using are so specific and so overused, if you are in a competitive market if you are caller number 10, the seller might know the script better than the agent calling.

    Specifically, there is a popular survey script that has been around the whole time I have been in the real estate industry. It is so overused, as soon as it starts the seller will often just hang up. Who has time to take the same survey 3 times? Who even has time to take it once?

With all of that being said, your script needs to be as easy as 1,2,3. It needs to flow like a natural conversations with the questions being relevant to the conversation. You can download my expired script at www.JasonMorrisBonus.com

Before we go through my script, let's talk about how do you get really good, really fast using scripts.

How to get really good using Scripts

1. The best way to really improve is to make real calls to sellers. I know a lot of agents get nervous and do not want to start out calling real leads on day 1, but the sooner you get started the faster the learning process will happen.

2. Roleplay. Getting a roleplay partner or even a couple of roleplay partners always helps. When you roleplay, make sure that you are both using the same script. If you aren't, it isn't as effective. As you are making calls and getting real seller objections, write them

down and work them out with your roleplay partner.

This process helps you build muscle memory and will really help you with working out how to overcome objections.

3. Being self aware of what you are saying and how you are saying it. Focusing on being positive, upbeat and confident. No one wants to work with an agent that sounds sad, negative and is not confident about the information they are giving.

4. Make calls with other Agents. This is a lot harder than it used to be with a lot of real estate brokerages not having physical offices. However, if you can find a partner to make prospecting calls with it, do it! Sitting in the same office listening to someone else make calls using the same script is really powerful!! It will shorten your learning curve tremendously.

Expired Script

Hey Mr. Seller, This is (your name) with (Realty Company). Do you still want to sell your house at (Address)? (yes)

How much will you take for it? (let them answer)

I saw you had it on the market, why do you think it didn't it sell? (let them answer)

I have been doing some research, I believe I know why your old agent didn't sell it. How soon do you want to get rid of this place? (let them answer)

Confirm information you see in MLS - example

So this home is a 3 bedroom 2 bath with a garage?
It has a new roof?
It is on a half of an acre?

Fantastic!

Will you be home this afternoon (or tomorrow, you state the time always)? (yes)
I am going to be in your area, can I stop by at 4pm? (ok) (try to set an appointment asap, other agents are calling)

I want to send you some information about me, so you know who will be stopping by your house? What is your email address? (send them your pre-listing package asap)

Confirm Your appointment and show up early!!

End of Script

***The purpose of your call is to set an appointment**

Your pre-listing package

A lot of people call this a "listing package," I prefer "pre-appointment package" when I am talking to clients. One thing that will help you all get more listings is to eliminate the word "listing" from your vocabulary when talking to sellers. Somehow that has become a bad word, and really it is just industry slang anyway. But when you are talking to Expired Listings they don't want to "list" because somebody they know has done that and it didn't work. Expireds don't want to list their house because they "listed" with the last agent and it didn't work out either. You want to talk about "selling" their home, getting their home "sold." And you want to talk about it confidently.

The Pre-appointment package is the #1 listing tool in my tool box. If I had to pick just one thing that has gotten me more listings that other agents over and over this is it!

A lot of agents get it wrong, and it will sound shocking to a lot of realtors, but we actually **DO NOT** sell houses. We sell a service that sells houses. It just so happens, we get paid on the performance of that service.

This pre-listing package will give you the framework for the home selling service you offer. Your goal in the business should be to set up your real estate practice to operate like a business. A lot of agents just run around constantly over promising and under delivering over and over to clients. The truth is they don't even know what services they are offering. But you guys are going to know exactly what you are offering! Because you are going to have a package that says you do.

My favorite line to use with sellers that are meeting with multiple agents is "So Mr. seller, I know you are meeting with another agent; what I want to do is send you my pre-appointment package, it tells about what my team and I do to sell homes. I would like you to request the other agents marketing plan also, that way you can put them side by side and compare the services we both offer."

When or if they say the other agent doesn't have one and it happens a LOT. My next line is always "Oh my gosh, Mr seller, I hope they aren't just going to put a sign out in your yard and pray something will happen?" That must be what they are going to do since they do not have a written plan? I find that in most markets, even the best, biggest agents don't have one.

Having a pre-appointment package is going to do 7 things for you

1. It is going to give you a lot of confidence. You have something in writing that is already prepared to give potential sellers. You won't have to fumble around and worry about what products or services did you forget to tell them about. They knew about you before you ever parked your car.

2. It is going to make you appear to be extremely professional. Chances are if you are talking to a FSBO or an expired listing they have already talked to a lot of agents. 99% of them had nothing at all to give them or send them about their services. You are going to look like you really have things together. You are a real estate agent with a plan.

3. It is going to establish expectations for

your client. If you do not want to do open houses, don't put it in the package. If you do have a great open house system that you get results from, you might want to include that. I would not include anything that you not are willing to consistently do for every single listing. If you put in your package you do open houses or you use flyer boxes, you better believe every seller is going to expect one.

4. You get a chance to show off your whole team. Now what I am calling a team is not what we commonly hear today referred to as a team. One particular franchise seems to have skewed the whole industry; what has happened is you have agents running around talking about "My team, " and they are referring to a group of 15 agents. The team I'm talking about is your BIC, your office staff and administration, the size of your office, the attorneys and vendors you work with, etc. This is the team that helps you get from listing agreement to closing. Even brand new agents have a team.

5. It saves time! You send your pre-listing package out usually the day before your appointment. Preferably by email. You ask them to look over it. You even remind them to look over it when you follow up and ask if they have any questions. Then when you get to the house, one of the first things you ask is "did you look over the information I sent you?" Even if they didn't look over it, they probably will tell you they did. This will pretty much completely eliminate the need for a formal presentation about the services you offer. The seller already knows what you are going to do.

One phrase I use when I'm sitting down in front of a seller client is "Looking at the pre-appointment package and information I sent over to you, you know we market 2 ways. #1 we market to the general public looking for our own buyers and #2 we market to other agents looking for agents with qualified buyers. Our goal is to get you as many qualified buyers as possible to look at your home."

6. It establishes value. When potential

clients look at this package, it looks like a lot of stuff. Most people don't understand the basic list of services we offer as agents can be extensive!! This is what this is, the basic list of services you are offering.

Everything from taking pictures, putting out a for sale sign, putting out a lock bock, notifying agents in your market and then the syndication your franchise or local MLS board offers is extensive. The basic list of services we all provide is mine blowing, a lot of it is done automatically or through the whole process, but sometimes even when I look at the list, I think "man I do a lot of stuff."

7. Your pre listing package also builds trust. It shows you are who you say you are. This is one of the biggest things often missing in our industry. The media was not very kind to real estate agents during the last downturn in the market. Plus there are a lot of weird scams now days.

I don't just use this tool for people I've set

appointments with. I use this to send to everybody!! This is my personal brochure that tells about me, my company and what we do to sell houses. Making a great looking pre-listing package that just sits on your computer doesn't do you any good at all! If you talk to a property seller, you need to ask them for an email address. If you talk to anybody else that mentions they are thinking about selling their home, ask for their email address. Send your pre-listing package to them as soon as you can.

The line that works best for me over and over is "I want to send you some information about my team and me, that way you know who you are talking to. What is your email?" 9 out of 10 people just give it to you. My next question is "is this your cell phone number I'm calling you on?" I'll talk more about why you ask for this when we talk about follow up.

I give away my free Pre-listing package template at JasonMorrisprelistingpackage.com.

Building your follow up system

What you need is massive deliberate follow-up.

I created a full years followup plan for seller leads you can get at www.FollowupMaster Dayplanner.com

You want to double your business, and you are already making calls, you need to double, triple and 10x your follow up. This is how you are going to increase the number of appointments and the number of expireds you are listing. Massive follow up!

In this chapter, I am going to tell you why follow-up makes the difference when getting listings and then I am going to walk you through my process to Design a massive follow-up system for sellers.

One thing I want to go ahead and get out of the way is, I do not automate a drip campaign. I think that is a huge mistake agents make. Everyone is looking for an easy way. There isn't one. There may be some things you can automate like follow up notifications, but a 15 or 20 email canned email sequence is not something that will work in today's market.

Most agents have a "catch you when I can" system, meaning they follow up if they don't have anything to do and they happen to see the person's name on their desk.
There is a "cool off factor" in our business. Most agents don't understand this, but there is a cool off factor in every business.

This is an example of what I am talking about

Let's say a driver sees a police officer on the side of the road. How long will that driver slow down?
1. 5 miles
2. 5 minutes
3. Less than a mile

Most of us will slow down for less than a mile. This is the cool off factor. People have very short memories. Most real estate agents are very bad at keeping up with people. With buyers and sellers when you are Out of sight you are out of mind.

I am going to tell you what most agents do, and then I am going to give you an example of what my follow up system looks like.

This is what most real estate agent follow up system looks like. So you just hung up with a fantastic potential client. You had a great meaningful conversation (by meaningful, I mean they told you all of their deep dark secrets about selling the house down to the penny of what they needed to walk away with and how he just got transferred with work and has to move). Now you are sure you are going to list this house, but this is a crazy week, and he says "call me on Monday."

How many times has that ever happened to you? I bet this sounds very familiar.
Well, today, the day you talked to him is Tuesday. So by Wednesday, he kind of cools off a little bit,(the cool off factor takes effect) he doesn't hear from you, no emails, no text, no pre-listing package. Thursday rolls around, he has talked to a couple more agents from his craigslist ad he threw up the night before. Now it is Friday, Mr. Seller does not remember your name. You haven't followed-up. Out of sight, out of mind.

So come Monday, 6 days later, when you call, he does not know who you are, never heard of you, he doesn't remember talking to you. There is so much clutter and competition out there, a week later (depending on the market) he talked to 10 other agents already. All of them used scripts and were better and more confident on the phone than you. You had 6 days where you gave an opening and let another agent get involved in the conversation you were having with that seller. By the time you talk to him, it has already been on MLS for 2 days.

So your job once you have a serious conversation with a listing prospect is to do 2 things.

#1 keep them hot on you - stay in front of them - Do not let them go
#2 keep them hot on selling their house

If you've built a good rapport, you do not want to lose that, and you need to keep that conversation going. Hopefully you made a good impression; hopefully you told him you were sending over your pre-listing package, and you actually had one to send over.

Hopefully you followed up by text as soon as you hit send on the pre-listing package.
Do not mail this package initially unless the seller still lives in 1982 where the internet didn't exist. By the time the mail gets there, you have given another agent a chance to step into the conversation! Mailing this package is the last resort to get it to them.

Now the whole real estate sales process in today's world revolves around trust and respect. I am a big believer we use to broker information. When I first started selling real estate we brokered information, 10 years ago we brokered information, now that information is widely available to the general public. Now we broker trust. Every minute, every day the prospect does not hear from you this trust and respect level you built on that initial call starts to fall off.

Now I want to tell you what my follow-up process would look like with this same seller. After I talk to a potential seller, I get their email - My favorite line I use is "Hey, Mr. seller, I want to send you over some information about me and my company, that way you know who you are talking to (or you know who is coming by your house). My pre-listing package goes out within an hour. It is all set up on my laptop. I just drag and drop it.

Then type up an email. Now that email is very important, you want it to reference the seller point of pain. The point of pain is the reason they told you they are selling. You want this email to be confident and strong. Do not write "I think we can sell your house" write "Our marketing works, I know we can sell your house." If you do not have confidence in yourself, why should they have confidence in you?

Then I text them as soon as I push send, with just a short text "Hey, this is Jason Morris, I want to make sure you got my email."

The next day, day #2 I'm calling him "hey I wanted to make sure you got my package and see if you have any questions about my company and me?" I answer any questions - I then try to close for an appointment again. I try to close for an appointment on every call.

Day #3 I call and say "I was on MLS this morning looking at homes in and around your neighborhood, is yours a 3br? (Confirm the stuff you guys talked about)". Next I confirm the price. Then, I try to set another appointment. "I know this week has been a little crazy for you, I know you have to get this place sold, so you can _____(whatever reason they told you). I would like to go ahead and meet you this weekend? Would Saturday morning or Sunday afternoon work for you?" I try to set the appointment again.

If they say no, I try to set a time and day for next week. If they say call me back on Monday, put them in your calendar for Monday. But send him over your net sheet - with a short email "hey I worked this net sheet up to give you an idea of what you will walk away with. I will bring all of the information with me when we meet next week."

So in this scenario between your initial call and your follow up call was 6 days.

My first follow was under an hour, my second one was under 24 hours. In the first 24 hours you sent an email, you sent a confirmation text, and you called to follow up. By Friday you have made 4 to 5 contacts. Other agents have made 1 call.

Plus every follow up call wasn't being pushy or

salesman-y, it was offering something of interest to them. I offered help each time. I always follow up with the mindset of helping and educating. As far as most people are concerned, by the time Monday rolls around I am working for them. I tell sellers "I do a lot of work before coming to someone's home."
I have never had anyone say "hey I didn't work with Jason because he just followed up too much, the guy kept me too informed."

Now make sure you use those motivating factors you talked about in the initial conversation.

Now what to do if you call Monday and you don't get them on the phone? Who has a great CRM they are using? If you don't have a CRM, get yourself a spiral notebook to start out with. You need something to keep up with all of your potential clients.

You need some sort of system to keep up with people.

You need to record every action you take. If you work on a CRM, you can automate your follow-up, and by automating, I am not talking about spam follow up. I am talking about it automatically schedules when you need to follow up.

So let's say Monday you can't get the seller on the phone. You need to text and email. "Hey, you wanted me to follow up with you today, just left you a voice mail. Give me a call at your earliest convenience.

Do you see where follow-up makes the difference? if you were that average agent competing for the listing with we, who do you think would get it?

If you can't get in touch with the person when you call, send an email and a text, for the first 10 days. You can go longer, but typically I have talked to most sellers within 10 days.

You need to vary your follow up times you are calling. By my follow up attempt 7 or 8 with no answer my messages are typically, "I have been trying to get in touch with you, do you still want to sell your house?"

What I want to do in this chapter is to help you design your follow up the system and what happens when you have had that initial conversation with them. I believe most listings will take 12 to 14 follow ups before setting the appointment and taking the listing. You can get lucky and get the listing sooner.

Here is your new follow-up system. Use this as a template and design your own. <u>DO NOT USE CANNED EMAILS FOR SELLER FOLLOW UP You can create templates to save</u>

Follow up #1

The first follow-up is your pre-listing package. If you guys do not have a pre-listing package, you need to put one together this week. This needs to be your top priority. It does not have to be elaborate. If you want to use my template go to JasonMorrisGroup.com and download it for free.

This one thing is going to change your business

When I don't set an appointment - I hold back the net sheet and paperwork - I use it for future follow up

Follow up #2

You text the seller to make sure they got your email. You need to burn it in your brain that your listing business revolves around your pre-listing package. This is the service you offer to sellers that other agents just don't offer. This is what you do to sell a house. As far as you are concerned, if another agent does not have a pre-listing package - they must just "poke and pray." I had an old broker in charge that use to say agents would "poke and pray" they would poke a sign in the front yard and pray it sells.

I have even told sellers this before when they tell me, they are meeting with multiple agents. "Have they sent you their marketing plan? (Answer: No) Oh my gosh, I hope they aren't going to just put a sign-out and hope somebody drives by?"

You may notice after a little while you just start getting call backs 100% from you sending out this package. More than likely you are the only agent sending this out.

Follow up #3 (the next day)

Call them and say "Hey, Mr. seller, I wanted to see if you have any questions about the information I sent you over. Answer any

- questions.

Every call I attempt to close for an appointment if I don't already have one. - I was doing some research - Are you going to be home on Thursday? (You specify the day?) I would like to stop by about 4 pm would that work for you?

You specify the day and time - because if you ask "what time will work for you? No time will ever work" they have to call you back. You give them an opening for one of the most common objections on the planet.

Why do you want to stop by - I can sell your house I want to meet you and take a look at it. You do want to sell your house right?

(They tell you it isn't a good time - I don't want to work with a realtor whatever - just say ok and move on to the next follow up)

Follow up #4 - Depends on their motivation as to when to follow up

Call - I was looking at homes on the market in your area. I want to send you over what I found. The market is changing (because it is always changing) stuff is always going on or off the market.

Try to close for the appointment.

I email the net sheet over to them with what is on the market. I will often detail out my email to some extent. Basically, I will put my whole pricing strategy into a short email.
(I always follow up the next day after I send this) every follow up is with their interest in mind, not your own.

Next day (I try to close again). Did you get the information that I sent you yesterday? Every time you send information, it gives you a chance to follow up the next day about what you sent.

Follow up 5 (usually a week or so will pass by)

Now by follow-up 5 - they probably know who you are - if they don't, then you really need to work on your presentation and emails, etc.

Follow up 5 is (I was in your neighborhood yesterday) It is more of a (I was thinking about you and your house). I know you want to sell your house because of _____ whatever they told you. I know I can sell your house. Let's meet this week. This call is typically a little more aggressive.

Follow up 6 (usually about a week)

So let's say follow up 5 you just really got shut down and didn't set the appointment.
This is the call you make where you say "Mr. seller, I am going to be in your area on Tuesday or whatever day. I wanted to see if Tuesday afternoon was a good time to meet.

Follow up 7 (holiday weekend)

Usually within a month or so you have some sort of holiday where people are off of work and kids are out of school. Use that holiday. Follow up the Monday before the holiday.

This follow-up will go something like "Hey, Mr. seller This weekend is "flag day, 4th of July or whatever holiday" Holidays are always big weeks for my follow up. "There will be a lot of people off of work and in town looking at houses. I don't want you to miss a buyer. I can get you in my schedule on Wednesday to get your home on the market, we might get it sold this weekend?"

Follow up #8 (my office done this)

This is why agents don't follow up, by this time, follow up is getting hard! Sometimes you have to get creative to continue making calls.

This calls usually goes something like this "Since I first talked to you, my office has had (_____ number of) properties go under contract. I really thought one of those would be yours. I know we can sell your house and get the price you are looking for. When are you ready for me to start working for you?"

Now if you are at a small office, you need to use the market statistics. "Since we started talking there has been x number of properties sold and x number that went under contract." Don't just use their neighborhood, use like a 1 or 2-mile radius depending on the density.

Follow up #9 (Your neighbor's house just sold)

This is a great follow up - "I just saw where the house down the street from yours just sold and they got _____ for it. I know you want _____ for yours?" Then tell them why or how their house was greater or worse than the one that sold.

Then ask for the appointment again

Follow up #10 (I wanted to see how things were going)

"Mr. seller I was going through some stuff in my office, and I wanted to see if you have sold your house or had an interested buyer yet?

I first talked to you about 45 days ago. I can help you, if I couldn't get you what you are looking for, I wouldn't keep calling you. When you want me to start working for you?"
By this time they know you. You have had 10 to 12 calls and follow-ups with them. You also have sent text and emails.

That is 10 follow-ups. This is the hard thing in the real estate business. The first call is easy, it's the 5th and 10th, and 15th follow up call that gets tough.

Don't take anything you are told from your follow up calls personal. Trust in the process, the follow-up process works.

Once you hit that 10th follow-up just cycle back through follow-ups 4 through 10 again.

Holidays are my favorite times to follow up!

Those steps 4 thru 10 - keeps cycling through those follow-up ideas and plans. You need to plan to follow up 15 to 20 times with a prospect before completely throwing them away or adding them to your long term nurture system.

5 years ago I would have told you that number was less, but I believe today as the market continues to improve, we are going to constantly have new agents jumping in and trying to get involved in the conversations we are having with our clients. That is how you need to think about your follow up, expect to follow up 15 to 20 times.

I know your state definition of what your client is, is different. But look at them as these are my clients and I am calling them because I want to help them, and I am the best person that can help them.

<u>5 Things you should not do with your follow-up</u>

1. Don't make your follow-up system too complicated. If it is too complicated, you will not do it.

2. Do not get too fancy. I know as agents we all love the latest and greatest toys and cell phones. However, most of our clients are not as up to date on technology as we are. If you are not getting responses from video text, my advice would be don't send video text. Your client demographic may be at an age where they don't know what to do with those texts when they get them.

3. Do not stop following up with a good prospect. I guarantee your competition is following up with your buyers and sellers right now. This is a marathon, not a sprint.

4. Do not try to use a canned drip campaign. Especially if it is with one of the more popular CRMs. Chances are, your client has already seen those emails, or they are just going to spam.

5. Do not forget to make notes with every follow-up. Use any motivating factors or information you can get on your next calls.

Using a Pricing Strategy

You have to have an easy way to explain your pricing strategy and a real strategy that makes sense. I hear agents talk about solds, solds, solds when pricing a house. I've got news for you, if you are pricing based on solds, then you are doing it wrong. You need to use an ACTIVE listing pricing strategy. I know a lot of you have never heard of this because no one talks about a real pricing strategy with clients. Most agents only talk about solds, they don't know any different.

I know you probably know how to log on to your local MLS and pull comps and properties that have sold. If you are in a market trending upward, you are probably constantly losing listings to an agent that are pricing properties higher than you are. Some of you may even have the mindset that FSBOs and expireds are all overpriced. A lot of agents are probably just getting lucky with their pricing, or pricing the house to get the listing.
In a market rapidly moving upward, taking a listing that is 5% to 10% higher than what you think it will sell for isn't a big deal. Lots of time

the market will catch up. In a trending down market, you have to do the same thing, but price it towards the bottom of what is available.

You have to price ahead of the market! On every listing presentation you need to make a business decision. That decision is, where is the best place for me to have a sign? You choices are the trunk of your car or a sellers from yard.

This is a pricing strategy that not only will get the house sold but will be a lot easier to explain to your sellers than basing your price off of homes that have sold.

The way you price ahead of the market is that you price based on the actives not based on solds. You want to price based on what the listing is actually competing against in today's market. Buyers buying today are looking at homes for sale and comparing them. They may want to buy a house for the price it sold for 6 months ago, but that house is already gone.

Most agents are pricing homes with solds and are usually underpricing their listings. Pricing based on solds is like driving looking in your rearview mirror, it makes no sense.

The house that sold last month or 6 months ago doesn't really matter. In the time frame, a serious buyer is really looking to buy, that house will probably never be available again and if it is, it's going to be at a higher price.

What you do is take the home and pull actual active listings that are comparables from inside the community and/or a radius around the home. If the home is a 3 bedroom 2 bath with a 2 car garage, look up homes that are 3 bedroom 2bath with a garage. Look up actual comparables. With custom homes, this is a little more difficult, but you just compare the homes real features to the features of other available homes.

Usually, unless their home is something very special, I want to be priced one of the lowest comparables in the area. Usually, if there are 10 homes in the area, I want to be one of the lowest 3 or 4, and I want to be able to pick out the reasons and features that make my listing better than those 3 or 4.

Those reasons could be anything you can really justify. Things like a new roof, a bigger home lot, more square footage. Things that are actually a plus.

You want to show up to your listing appointment very prepared. I will often print out comparables and make notes on them so I can quickly justify why a house is better or worse than the one I'm trying to list.

The more you prepare with comparables and details about the active listings, the more likely it will be that you will get the listing.

I always pull the active listing real quick before putting together the net sheet. You want everything you do with pulling comparables to support whatever prices you have on your net sheet. Don't show up with a net sheet and then comparables that tell a completely different story.

Now you guys have a Pricing strategy.

Let's talk about how you set up your net sheet.

Setting up your net sheet

If you are not using a net sheet, you are doing yourself and your clients a dis-service. This sheet eliminates so many objections. This is a vital part of what I typically send over to clients and go over in the listing appointment.

This is so your client can actually see exactly what they are going to put in their pocket before their mortgage is paid off. No matter what people tell you, they know roughly what their mortgage balance is, but typically we don't know. That's ok though, we are just giving them an idea what they will get after real estate commission, attorney (title company) fees and any other common charge comes out of the gross. Often times property sellers have these crazy ideas about what it cost them to use an agent, the net sheet just lays it all out.

I usually do 3 columns, with the price I want to list their home in the middle. So I set it up column 1 is the low column, column 2 is where I want it priced, column 3 is usually the high end of what I think the property will sell for.

You should have an idea of what the dollar amount is your client wants to walk away with from the sale. If it is reasonable or low, I try to make sure the net amount in at least one of the columns. If the price they are needing is way more than what the market will bring, you probably shouldn't be going on the appointment.

I do have times where I set up an appointment, then call the person back later that day, after pulling comparables and setting up a net sheet and I just tell them "Hey, Mr seller I told you I could get you 100,000, I've been doing some research, I can't get you that price, I can only get you _____. Sometimes, they already know this and tell you "Ok that's fine" and you go list the property. Sometimes you just end up canceling.

Different markets may have different fees. These are typical fees. You are planning and preparing them for a smooth closing. If they have title issues or problems, the attorney might charge more. But don't worry about that, for the purpose of your net sheet, you are assuming this is a typical transaction with no issues.

In My market I include in each column, you can modify this to fit your market

1. The sales price - what I think the property will sell for

2. Attorney or title company fees - you should have your go-to attorney office or title company you work with. Typically they charge the same fee for a seller no matter what the size of the transaction. Locally the attorney I work with charges $350 for seller transactions. I typically put $400 in this block, everyone is always happy when things are cheaper

3. Transfer taxes. In our market, we call these deed stamps, and they are about $4 per $1,000 of the sales price. Every market has some version of this. Break it down and make it simple to understand. I usually provide a high estimate.

4. Admin/courier fees - it never fails, every closing I do there is some sort of $50 fee the attorney adds like this. I just include it in the net sheet so it is expected.

5. Commission rate - don't forget about this one

6. Termite Letter - In our market the seller typically pays for the termite inspection. It's only about $80 to $100. In other markets, you will have other things.

7. Misc - I always put $1,000 Misc in the spreadsheet. This is for 1 big reasons, it gives you a cushion for repairs or a home warranty. It seems there is always something that I don't know about. A $35 mortgage satisfaction letter or an HOA transfer fee. I always mention this to sellers and tell them "I would rather give you a number a little lower on this sheet and have you show up to closing putting a few dollars extra in your pocket." Everyone always likes that.

During the listing appointment, I go through the items on the net sheet. I don't go into a lot of detail, but I point out everything.

When putting together your net sheet you need to make it as simple as you possibly can! It needs to be very simple so anybody can understand it! I see some of these net sheets in other training programs that are way over the top. Those are fine if you want to use those for personal use.

If you remember the beginning of this book, most of the people you are going to be meeting have probably never sold a home before. Even the most experienced sellers we typically run into haven't been through the home-selling process more than a few times.

We forget that we see this stuff every day. A lot of us live and breathe real estate. Your average client isn't like this at all. Remember this is one of their first transactions, if not their first.

Plus you don't want something very elaborate that creates a lot of work for you every time you send it out.

If it is too complicated, you just will not do it.

Listing Paperwork Presentation

I know some of you are probably thinking, why did Jason want to include a chapter about contracts and listing paperwork. Jason doesn't work in my state, or my broker constantly has classes going over this. They do, they teach you what it says, but they don't often teach you how to present it to clients.

This is something I see over and over with agents. Your broker probably has classes talking about all your contracts and listing paperwork, and they go down thru this stuff with you word for word. What I see is most agents turn around and go thru it with their client's word for word.

Well, the first thing is when most brokers have this class they tell you all the scary stuff that is in these documents. Let's face it, there is some scary stuff in there. Your average client does not deal with legal documents every day. Then when they have a question about a section most agents tell their clients these same crazy stories their broker told them.

Typically in most real estate agent contracts there is the whole Megan's law section about sex offenders, a section about how we can sue the client if they don't pay us, a section about how we are not responsible for anything, a whole mediation clause and probably a lot more scary stuff in some states. There are a lot of big words, scary things and for most people, this is one of the first times they have ever seen any of it. It is a legal document. Nobody likes going over legal documents and they are boring. Not to mention, most people think it is insulting for someone to read word for word 6 or 10 pages to them.

The mistake I see agents make over and over is that they don't really know what the paperwork says or how to explain it easily. In the state of South Carolina, there are only about 4 or 5 contracts, and forms we use and most agents and even some brokers do not know what they really say or how to easily explain them to a client.

When you're meeting your clients, you want to be able to completely, and effectively get through the paperwork as quickly and painlessly as possible. You want to do this on a very simple level. I can't help you guys with this in other states, I only know about the South Carolina paperwork.

You should take your listing paperwork and a sheet of paper and writing out a short explanation of each section or each. Just paraphrase it. You should not go through it word for word with a client. When you do go through it word for word, it really makes you look like you don't know what it says. Send the whole listing package with the pre-listing package and they can read it beforehand if they want to.

I will give you an example, the South Carolina state contract has a section about Megan's Law which is the sex offender registry. They have a 2-inch paragraph that basically says "if you care about the sex offender registry and who is on it there is a website you can look it up on."

It is so much less painful to give that short explanation. You can do this for each contract while still making sure you go over all the important parts.

I really believe a lot of agents don't get listings because they don't know how to properly explain the paperwork and they over complicate it.

If you are going to list appointments, the seller's love you and all of a sudden you go through the paperwork, and they say "we need to think about it." There is a good chance it is how you are presenting the paperwork.

Write out your script and practice explaining and presenting it. You closing ratios at listing appointments will go through the roof.

You should also do this with your buyer contracts too and any other regularly used form your state has.

I include my listing paperwork in every pre-listing package that I send out. The version I email is just a clean copy that has everything filled in except the seller's name, property details, price, and dates.

You want to make sure you have it highlighted everywhere the client needs to initial and sign.

I send this for 2 reasons.

1. I want them to know for sure I am planning to meet them to do business. I don't go to people's homes to preview properties. I go to get their home on the market and start the process of looking for a buyer.

2. I want them to be familiar with the paperwork. Most people when they look at your pre-listing package they will at least pull it up and skim through it.

Now when I show up to the listing appointment, I always have the paperwork completely filled out. Except for price, I like to fill that in when I'm sitting in front of the client. I am 100% prepared when I get to someone's house.

I know there are a lot of agents that like to do this all digital, the sales process is not nearly as effective sitting in front of people asking them to digitally sign paperwork on an iPad. Plus it's hard for most people who are not tech savvy to scroll through and look back over everything if needed. This whole process is so much easier if you print out your paperwork. Your conversion rate when doing face to face listing appointments will go up with printed paperwork.

Also, I find people are a lot less likely to want to negotiate commission rates when the commission blank is pre-filled in.

I cannot stress enough, you must show up completely prepared for your appointment. Like, prepared to the point it may seem ridiculous. I have created a ritual around this myself. It only takes me about 10 minutes or so to put the whole package together.

Set it all up with your Gmail canned emails and on the desktop of your computer so you can just drag and drop everything into the email.

If you make it all too difficult you just won't do it.

Listing appointment

My listing presentation starts before I get to the house. I really want to put my whole system into perspective for you all. The last chapter of this book I am going to use to tie everything together.

When the market really booms (which at the time of this being published it is going crazy), we are going to start seeing downward pressure on real estate commissions. Our services are not going to be as needed or in as much demand. You are going to need to get better at relaying what your value proposition is. Why should they hire you? Why should they write you a check at closing for, in most markets is, upwards of $5,000 to 10,000 or more.

The way you are going to do this is by making sure your listing process is in place and making sure you know how to overcome the most common objections. Your listing process should eliminate most, if not all of those objections.

I started in the real estate business going on 14 years ago. There were really the same objections then as there is now. Nothing has changed. There are not classes that teach sellers new objections.

Now there is such a thing as a condition. A condition is different. For example, a condition is something in most cases that is true, it's not just a smoke screen that a seller throws up to get you off the phone and to quit calling them. A condition would be like, a tree fell on my roof, and you can't really list a house with a tree on the roof.

Maybe the house is really being fully rehabbed. Maybe they really are sick or injured. Use your best judgment to decide what it really is, a condition or an objection.

The number 1 objection we all get when we make calls, I feel like we can agree on this one, is real estate commission related. The reason why we are having this objection is because we are focusing the conversation on what we are making off the transaction and putting in our pockets versus what the seller is walking away with.

If you start focusing that conversation on what do they want to walk away with you are going to start having different conversations. The way you are going to start having different conversations is by asking different questions. (I mentioned this earlier)

For example: when we initially talk about price with a seller, we should only talk about what they want to walk away, not about what you want to list it for. "Mr. seller, how much do you want to walk away with at closing?" "What do you want for the property after everything's said and done? Attorney fees and everything"? "What do you want to put in your pocket at closing?" these are all great questions. Once I hear their answer, I immediately say "that is fantastic" I then close for an appoint.

The reason I mention this in this chapter is because this is vital information you need for the appointment and for your process.

Once you know what they want, the rest is pretty easy. You just build your net sheet and listing price backward around netting them the amount they want to leave closing with. It is just that simple. Use your net sheet. Make your net sheet very simple. Like 2nd-grade level math simple. A lot of these people you work with, they are not like us, (remember) this is probably one of their first home selling transactions. Even experienced sellers in most cases, doing general brokerage, haven't sold more than a couple of properties.

Chances are the advice they are getting is from somebody that knows even less than they do.

You want everything to be as easy as possible to understand and explain. If you cannot explain your home selling process and how you sell homes, <u>it will affect your ability to list homes.</u>

So this what your listing presentation should look like. Let me first put this all into context for you.

So you made the call and set the appointment. You sent over your pre-listing package. For you guys that haven't gotten yours together, this should be a priority. You can get my template at JasonMorrisgroup.com

Your listing package tells about what you do to sell a home. Like I told you earlier, it is my belief, we don't really sell homes. What we sell is a service that sells homes. This pre-listing package tells about that service. It is simple 10 to 12 pages, lots of graphics, not tons of text. If yours is 50 pages and you wonder why nobody looks at it, it's because it is 50 pages. If you get a 50-page pdf that is all 10 point text, no pictures what will you typically do with it? Especially if it is something, you were not really looking for. You just delete it or forget about it.

You want to make sure they get this. Text them, call them follow up and make sure they received it. See if they have any questions. If you are having trouble with follow-up, reference the follow-up chapter earlier in this book.

Then from here on out, the way you need to describe that document when you talk to that seller is "you got my pre-appointment package, it has our full marketing plan. So you know we market 2 different ways. We market to the general public looking for our buyers we can show your house too, then we market to other real estate agents looking for agents that have qualified buyers". Anytime you talk about buyers coming to their house specifically refer to them as "qualified buyers," we bring qualified buyers, we show your house to qualified buyers. We want to get your home in front of as many qualified buyers as quick as we can, our pre-appointment package talks about our plan to do that."

So as soon as you show up. Always, always, always show up early. Like 10 to 15 minutes early. If your appointment is at 2 pm and you show up at 2:15, you already look bad.

As you go on more appointments, you will get more comfortable going through people's homes.

You guys need to go on as many appointments as you possibly can. One of 2 things happens at every appointment. #1 you might list their house. #2 you practice your dialogues and presentation.

So I walk into the seller's house. I introduce myself, I shake everyone's hand. I hand them a couple of business cards. I make a little small talk. The weather is nice and that sort of stuff. i usually compliment them on something random.

Then I confirm (again) they received my pre-appointment package. Then I confirm the price

THEY want to walk away with! This is the price **THEY** gave me on the first call, this is **NOT** the listing price. Right after I do that, I usually say something like "so who wants to give me the tour?" I walk through the house. As I am walking through, I try to point out anything that I think will be an issue and I talk about everything as if we are already working together. For example "hey when **WE** bring a buyer, when **We** do _____, everything is **WE**.

I typically look for things that jump out at me and make me think, "wow, this is a problem". Water spots on the ceiling, soft places on the floor, dirty carpet, and dirty walls. I try not to be too critical of anything. I never point out a problem without asking about it and offering a solution. Chances are, they know about the problem already.

That solution I typically offer can be a couple of different things "are you guys going to fix this?" For example, "do you think these carpets will clean up or do you think they need to be replaced?" Wait for their answer and ask if they want to have it done or offer a credit. If they say they don't want to do anything, I would move on from it, but make a mental note.

Once I get through the house, I always tell people, "I do a lot of research before I come to your home. Can we sit at your kitchen table and look and look at what I found?" I always sit at the same place at the kitchen table. It is really where I am most comfortable spreading out paperwork and going through it.

Then I confirm (AGAIN) what they wanted for the home.

I pull out my comparables I found with my active pricing strategy and explain to them how I price property. Which pricing based on active competition makes a whole lot more sense than pricing based on homes that sold 6 months ago.

Next I pull out my net sheet (hopefully you prepared your active comparables and net sheet so that they support each other as I talked about in the previous chapter). I go down through it quickly. I typically circle the net number at the bottom of the sheet and ask "you wanted _____ and at this price, you will net _____, would that work for you?"
I wait for their answer then say "I brought my paperwork with me how about I go through it?" Then I pull out my listing paperwork (that is

already filled out) and go through my paperwork presentation we talked about early.

Typically in most appointments, I ask if they have any questions and just hand them an ink pen.

Most appointments last 30 to 40 minutes. A problem I had in the past is, I would do these really long presentations. I would leave without paperwork signed thinking "wow those people liked me and I am listing their home". Then a week later they would list their home with someone else. My appointment to listing ratio was almost embarrassing.

I learned that when I shortened up my presentation, my closing ratios went up. Then when I started using a pre-listing package, a net sheet and preparing as much as possible they went up even more.

If you are doing 2 hour presentations and not getting the appointment, it is because you are overstaying your welcome. Shorten up your appointments and you will start leaving with more paperwork signed.

Remember these people only have you in their

home because they think you can sell it and the only reason you are really there is because it is your job. Typically these people have a problem and they believe selling their home will fix that problem. That is the only reason you are there. It is great to be friendly and build rapport but a listing appointment is not a social visit.

Putting my whole system together

I feel like not enough books do this. They give you a system in parts then don't really tie it all together for you.

Things you need to make my system work is:

1. Lead sources - you have to have Expired leads
2. Scripts
3. Pre-listing Package - you need to put this together ASAP
4. Active pricing strategy
5. Paperwork Presentation
6. Net Sheet - you have to put together a net sheet
7. Role Play partner - go to Real estate agents that REALLY work (facebook group) and make a post looking for one.

Here are the steps you need to follow

1. Make yourself a regular schedule to follow. Actually, put "Calling expireds" into your schedule. If you do not put it on your schedule, it will not get done

2. Get a role play partner and start using my script. Both of you need to use the same script. If you do not know where to find a role play partner go to my group Real Estate Agents that REALLY work www.Facebook.com/groups/Realestateagentsthatreallywork and make a post in there that you are looking for one

3. Subscribe to Redx Expireds (for a discount use the link www.JasonMorrisExpiredLeads.com or call them and tell them you have my book) Start making calls as soon as possible. Don't make excuses like "I want to practice first" or "I want to get good with the script." The thing that will make you really good with the script is actually making calls.

4. As soon as you get an appointment send them out your pre-listing package. And text them to confirm they received it

as soon as you sent it.

5. Follow up the next day and see if they have any questions.

6. If you don't set an appointment - follow up

7. Show up at their house and follow the steps in my Listing Appointment chapter.

It is really that easy!

I wish you all the best of luck. If I can answer any questions for you, send me an email at JasonMorrisCoaching@gmail.com or visit my website JasonMorrisGroupCoaching.com

Tools and tips to Make this easier

1. Get a service to give you the numbers to call expired listings. It takes to long to try to look them all up yourself. Plus the harder you make it, the least likely it is that you will do it.

2. Consistency is the key. If you prospect consistently, you will go on a consistent number of appointments and take a consistent amount of listings. Consistent listings will lead to consistent contract and consistent paychecks!
The more often you make calls, the better you will get at it. It is like playing golf or playing any other sport. The first day, everyone sucks.

3. Use a dialer. I know a lot of agents do not want the extra expense starting out. I fought that too for a while. But when I tried it out, the time you save and the elimination of procrastinating outweighs the cost at least 100x.

I always recommend using Storm Dialer because it fully integrates with Redx. If you try to get expired data from one place and a dialer from another, it just creates another step in your prospecting. For me, it typically just makes it harder to get started every day.

4. Get yourself a notebook for your hot leads. I know, you are probably saying "but I got a CRM". I said the same thing. The problem was, sometimes I would schedule follow up time for myself and I would get distracted and spend an hour playing around in a CRM that had a million options.

   A $4 notebook from Wal-mart is one of the best tools I have. I can write notes while I am on the phone. I don't have to dig through my 10,000 contact database to find that one name. Plus it just helps me stay focused. It is simple.

5. Keep your system simple. The issue many of us have is we try to find an easy way. I have included a chapter with ideas about other things you can do to

follow up and contact expireds, but really the more simple your process is, the better.

Bonus: The $100,000 notebook plan

I wanted to put an action plan together for you that has been successful for me over and over.

This is not a guarantee, this is a plan that will require you to work. Everytime I have gotten in a little slump prospecting or needed to get my business jump started again after taking some time off, this has worked for me.

The numbers I am going to use are from my own personal experience.

Before we get started there are a few things you need:

1. A subscription to an expired service that will give you new plus old expired leads (preferably redx - www.JasonMorrisExpiredLeads.com)
2. A dialer will make things a whole lot easier (I recommend the redx Storm

Dialer)

For the purpose of easy math we are going to say that every listing you take and sell is worth an average of $5,000 in commission to the listing agent. That is about a $165,000 home with a 3% commission going back to the listing agent.

So for this plan we are needing to add to our "hot lead" notebook 20 leads that we have had meaningful conversations with. I talked about this in the section titled "How your expired listing business will look". You can find lead sheets in the back of this book.

Step 1: Get Leads

Contact Redx about getting every expired and FSBO lead from your market for the last 12 to 18 months. I would not be scared to go back 2 years. A lot of these old leads still want to sell, it just expired and in most cases the market has changed enough that they can possibly get more money for their home.

Step 2: Schedule time for Massive Action

•

This plan isn't for the agents out there that are not committed. This plan is about adding an extraordinary amount of future income to your business, you are going to have to do a lot of work for a short period of time.

Look and see how many leads you have. For this example, I am going to say you got about 2,000 expired/fsbo leads from the last 12 to 24 months. Some markets may vary, some markets you might get more. Call Redx, tell them I sent you and ask their tech support. They are super helpful.

What we are trying to figure out is, how long will it take you to go through all of these leads, calling them.

If you are hand dialing, in the past I have been able to dial 40 numbers an hour. However, that pace is wasting NO time. It is being super focused and dialing like a crazy person.

At 40 dials per hour 2,000 calls would take you about 50 hours.

This is where a dialer really comes in handy. With a dialer you can comfortably dial about 80 numbers per hour. You are not going to procrastinate over the next call or even have to leave voicemails. You can record 1 message and have it auto drop them for you. The extra expense will save you a significant amount of prospecting time.

At 80 dials per hour, 2,000 calls take about 25 hours.

We are going to assume you have a dialer and you could show up to the office, bringing your lunch and probably get through these 2,000 number in about 3 days.

Step 3. Making the calls and a script

These calls will be tough, you will get a lot of rejection in a short period of time, but you are going to add a ton of future business quickly. Plus these old leads, do not have many agents calling them!

Your initial script will be very simple, here is an example:

Hey Mr/Mrs seller. This is (Your Name) with (realty company). I was calling you about (property address), would you still be interested in selling it?

They will say "yes" or "no". If they say no, thank for their time. If they say "yes" continue with the expired script you will find in the back of this book.

If they give you a "Maybe" answer, take it as a yes and continue the script.

What I have found when I do this is that about 1% to 1 ½% of your list will still be interested in selling their house or doing something with a property in the next 30 to 90 days.

If you call this list and then all the ones you didn't get to talk to, you call them a 2nd and 3rd time, you will get an additional ½% to 1% that will want to sell their house in the next 30 to 90 days.

So a list of 2,000 leads on the low end will give you, on the low end, about 20 hot seller leads. Based on my experience calling that 2,000 person list 2 to 3 times during a 1 week period you could fill your notebook with 40 to 50 hot seller leads.

The problem with this plan is, most agents will not do it!

Step 4. Follow up

Now that you have sorted through the massive lead list, your job is to follow up with these leads. Afterall, that is our job right?

By following up, you need to have a focused follow up plan where you are touching base with them at least once a week.

****

Following this plan and doing this monthly, even if you just make the calls for 1 day, would potentially be HUGE for your business.

I met an agent about 10 years ago that followed a similar plan and for 1 weekend out of each month, he scheduled 3 days of calls. He told me that he rented a cheap hotel room so that he had no distractions from the office, his family or anything. He would make calls for about 10 hours a day in the hotel room and then go home.

He would take all of the leads he got from those leads and the ones he had from the months before and just follow up with them.

The rest of the month, his work schedule was super easy. He scheduled an hour to two hours a day (Monday through Friday) for follow up calls and then just went on appointments. He typically carried around 20 to 30 active listings and they were all taken care of by a licensed assistant and a showing service.

This guy had the hours of what most of us would consider being a part-time agent, but he was pretty consistently making about $250,000 a year.

Other expired Contact and Follow up Ideas

In this book we have focused on picking up the phone and calling expired listing leads. The telephone is still the number 1 way to communicate.

I did want to include a chapter giving you a few ideas on other ways to attempt to contact sellers that I have personally tried, or have interviewed agents for my group coaching, that are working on a high level.

1. Direct Mail. The key to direct mail is frequency when mailing to expired listings. Just sending out one letter on the day it expired will be tough. These listings are getting stacks of mail from agents on the day they expire. You may need to send a significant amount of follow up pieces of mail to an expired listing to get a response.

2. Voicemail drops. Services like Slydial, will allow you to record 1 voicemail and

have it bypass the ringing and actually show up in the voicemail boxes of 1000s of numbers without any of them ringing.

You will get call backs from this. The difficult part is figuring out who is calling you back.

3. Facebook ads. Using a service like Redx Oynx you get a lot of email addresses. Facebook is constantly changing its targeting options but you can often get enough data to specifically target a lot of individual sellers. This could potentially be a great strategy in addition to making calls and mail, just to stay in front of sellers in a specific area.

4. Text Messages. I have had a lot of success following up with text. Especially sellers that were tough to get back in touch with. I am not a fan of mass texts, but the coolest cell phone feature I have found, is Android allows you to schedule text. I am sure Iphone has something similar.

5. Door Knocking. The expired without phone numbers are probably not getting

called by anyone. It never hurts to just stop by and knock on the door and if they aren't home leave something

This is just a few things I have seen working successfully on a high leave. Meaning you can replicate them over and over to get a conversion ratio.

Thank You

Thank you for buying my How to Be an Expired Master Book. I hope you enjoyed it and it makes your business more profitable.

Please leave me a 5 star review on Amazon.

Made in United States
Troutdale, OR
03/27/2024

18746688R00077